A Nut in a Cup

Illustrated by Karen Bell

Editorial Offices: Glenview, Illinois • Parsippany, New Jersey • New York, New York
Sales Offices: Parsippany, New Jersey • Duluth, Georgia • Glenview, Illinois
Coppell, Texas • Ontario, California

A pup dug in the mud.

The pup dug up a nut.

Pop! The nut hit a log.

Diz sat on the log.

The nut went up.

Pop! The nut hit the cup.

A pup dug in the mud.

Diz sat on the log.

A nut was in the cup.

8